THE RAILRO

AD SCENE

WILLIAM D. MIDDLETON

Golden West Books
San Marino, California

END PAGE – FRONTIS – TITLE PAGE ILLUSTRATIONS

Title Page – Bound for East End Yard with a switch run from Duluth, Northern Pacific class W-3 Mikado No. 1805 heads out of Superior, Wisconsin, on New Year's Day – 1957. *Frontis* – On a bitter January morning in 1949 Milwaukee Road Mikado No. 471 brings the Chicago overnight freight into Madison, Wisconsin. *Front End Page* – Distinctively Delaware & Hudson were the railway's 40 handsome J class 4-6-6-4 Challengers, constructed by Alco's Schenectady works between 1940 and 1946. On a spring day in 1950, J class No 1504 pounds upgrade out of the Mohawk Valley at South Schenectady with 73 cars of westbound freight for the Susquehanna Division. *Rear End Page* – Clattering eastward across the vastness of the North Dakota prairie as Oakes-Staples (Minnesota) local train No. 112, the Northern Pacific's gas-electric car B-18 paused at Wyndmere in the early spring of 1959 to handle mail and express traffic. In the distance an eastbound Soo Line freight waits impatiently for the "train-in-one-car" to clear the crossing.

Golden West Books

P.O. BOX 8136 • SAN MARINO, CALIFORNIA • 91108

Bound north for Superior and Duluth, Great Northern's *Gopher* races through the Twin Cities campus-University of Minnesota.

TABLE OF CONTENTS

With three Union Pacific E units on the head end, east-bound train 102, the *City of San Francisco*, whips through a fresh November snowfall at Forreston, Illinois, on the last lap of its journey into Chicago over Milwaukee Road rails.

FOREW

From successive generations of Americans the railroad has exacted an almost universal fascination. It is not difficult to understand why this has been so. Prime mover in the civilization of a continent and the building of a nation, and, in its time, the indispensable mover of goods and purveyor of personal transportation, the railroad wove a net of steel rails that bound America together and brought a breath of far and fascinating places to the most commonplace of lives. Touching every life, the railroad could not be ignored.

Even more captivating, perhaps, has been the sheer physical impact of the sound and sight of massive machinery in motion that the railroad brought close to hand in a manner totally unlike any other industry. Shrieking, clanging, roaring, and pounding its way through town and countryside, the railroad embedded itself in the subconsiousness of every American; one could never be indifferent to its presence.

Assuredly, the railroad scene of every generation has offered much of fascination. But I am inclined to the view that my generation has witnessed one of the most exciting periods of all in almost a century and a half of North American railroading, for we have seen some of the most fundamental changes in the technology of the railroad since the very origin of the flanged wheel on steel rail itself.

Confined by such fixed dimensions as a 4 foot 8½ inch track gauge and a standard coupler height, the railroad of necessity has always been evolutionary in its development. Yet so sweeping have been the changes of the last quarter century in the railroad's motive power, equipment, and very methods of merchandising transportation, that it is difficult to avoid the use of the term "revolutionary."

If by no means the only change of consequence, certainly nothing in railroading's era of change was more widely remarked than the death of steam, which had served the railroad since its very beginnings a century and a quarter before. Perhaps the ultimate total victory of the diesel-electric could have been foretold as early as 1934, when the *Zephyr* made its epochal nonstop Denver-Chicago run; certainly no later than 1939, when Electro-Motive's prototype FT road freight diesel set out on its barnstorming tour that broke steam's tonnage records from San Bernardino to Boston. But the issue was not to be decided that easily, and because it was not, the years immediately after the war were exciting ones at trackside.

Substantial numbers of modern steam locomotives had been delivered during the war, and there was a considerable body of opinion within the industry that had by no means accepted the invincibility of the diesel. Indeed, deliveries of new steam power to a few die-hard coal roads continued beyond 1950. Thus it was in the immediate post-war years that such experiments as poppet valve-equipped 4-8-4's, steam turbines, and rigid frame four cylinder designs were watched every bit as closely as the latest models from the diesel erecting halls at La Grange and Schenectady. And in 1946, when New York Central's Paul Kiefer matched his Niagaras against the latest Electro-Motive passenger diesels in through operation between Harmon and Chicago that saw the incomparable 4-8-4's running up in excess of 27,000 miles a month, the results were studied and debated throughout the industry.

But by the early 1950's steam versus diesel was no longer a subject that could be seriously argued, and it remained only to the faithful to record steam's last years. And frequently glorious ones they were! Acting as a buffer between inadequate diesel rosters and traffic peaks, modern steam power continued to wheel merchandise tonnage across Midwestern flatlands, forwarded the wheat rush over the prairies, rolled ore trains grossing better than 18,000 tons off the Mesabi Range to the Lakehead, and charged the mountain grades of the Far West until almost the end of the decade.

This, however, is not just a book about steam engines; too many others have been over that ground already. It is my view, rather, that there is much of interest to be found in railroading beyond that of steam alone; that the diesel that has taken its place exerts a powerful fascination all its own. Surely few can be indifferent to the whine of multiple freight units leaning on the dynamic brakes as they ease westbound tonnage down Cajon, the chant of V-16 diesels as a string of Geeps accelerate a manifest out of town, or the impact of a trio of E units leading 20 cars through an interlocking plant at 90 mph. And the continuing change wrought by the likes of second generation diesels, unit trains, the awesome dimensions of the super freight cars of the 1960's, or the promise of 160 mph M.U.'s under Penn Central catenary, guarantee that the fascination of the railroad will be an enduring one.

This book, then, is intended to be a pictorial representation of the total railroad scene — of engines and cars, of passenger trains and freight trains, of railroad people and railroad places — as I have recorded it on film over a period of two decades since the late 1940's. No claim of geographical balance or all-inclusiveness is made — what I have seen has been too limited by time and circumstance for that — but it is hoped that the photographs within this volume are at least representative of their time.

One who sets out to edit, caption, and lay out a volume devoted to his own photographs faces certain hazards. It is difficult to be either objective or selective about one's own work, and consequently the most rigid sort of self discipline must be imposed lest repetitiousness set in and what was meant to be an album become a scrap book. The degree of success I have had must be left to the reader to judge.

For their material assistance in the preparation of this volume I acknowledge with sincere thanks the contributions of Fred W. Schneider, III, who processed most of the prints for this book with a rare combination of technical skill and subject sensitivity; Al Rose, whose halftones and presswork know few peers; and finally, publisher Donald Duke, who encouraged its preparation, aided in countless ways in readying the book for the press, and, perhaps most important of all, assumed the risk of its publication.

WILLIAM D. MIDDLETON

Ewa, Oahu, Hawaii
November 1968

There was a time when New England and New Englanders occupied a commanding position in the affairs of North American railroading. During much of the 19th century Boston was the nation's railroad financial capital, and the decisions of Hub City bankers affected the destinies of railroads half a continent away. From hardy New England stock came such towering figures in railroad construction and management at Collis Huntington, Grenville Dodge, Austin Corbin, Henry Plant, and Dan Willard.

The region's carriers, in the century now past, occupied no less eminent a place. At a time when such an enterprise seemed sheer folly, the indomitable builders of the Fitchburg drove their great bore through Hoosac Mountain to create one of the railroad wonders of the 19th century; the New York, New Haven & Hartford Railroad paid 10 percent dividends without fail for decades on end; and such crack flyers as the Boston & Maine-Maine Central *Mt. Desert Limited* and the New York & New England's *White Train* were among the vanguard of the great luxury limiteds that were to represent the ultimate in civilized overland transportation in North America for more than half a century. If, in

Laying a pall of smoke across the Green Mountain countryside, Central Vermont Mountain No. 601 bridges the White River north of White River Junction, Vermont, with the New York-Montreal *Ambassador* one splendid autumn afternoon in October of 1949.

our time, the glory years of New England railroading were long past, there remained much of uncommon interest. While financial adversity prevented widespread motive power modernization during the several decades preceeding dieselization, New England was none the less the birthplace of modern steam power, in the person of Boston & Albany's celebrated 2-8-4 Berkshires, and its principal carriers acquired modest numbers of high performance steam locomotives of real distinction, most notably Boston & Maine's P-4 class Pacifics and R-1 class Mountains, each of which assuredly represented one of the handsomest designs of its particular wheel arrangement ever constructed; Central Vermont's massively proportioned 2-10-4 Selkirks; or the New Haven's huge I-5 4-6-4's.

In the era of dieselization and streamliners, too, the

New England roads were not without their pioneering moments. If it failed to follow up an early start, Boston & Maine was in the forefront of the streamliner era with its *Flying Yankee* near-duplicate of the original Burlington *Zephyr* of 1934. New Haven installed a 600 h.p. yard diesel as early as 1931 and was among the first roads to embark on large scale dieselization of main line passenger and freight traffic with a fleet of 2,000 h.p. dual service Alco-GE road units acquired in 1940. Not long afterward B&M was among the early roads to install the revolutionary Electro-Motive FT diesel that pioneered widespread freight dieselization on North American railroads. And even more recently, during the 1950's, New England lines became some of the most extensive operators of the Budd Rail Diesel Car.

CANADIAN NATIONAL IN NEW ENGLAND . . .

Conceived in the 19th century as a link between the wharves of Boston and the Great Lakes, the Central Vermont Railway ended in the current century as the Canadian National's gateway into New England. (Above) Autumn leaves had begun to turn on the Vermont hills on the first day of October 1949 as CV 4-8-2 No. 601 came pounding across the White River bridge with the *Ambassador* from Montreal. (Right) After turning over its coaches and parlor cars to the connecting Boston & Maine at White River Junction, the handsome Mountain retired to the nearby engine terminal for servicing prior to a late afternoon departure with the *Ambassador's* northbound opposite number. (Below) Ready for road freight assignments, a pair of Consolidations flank one of CV's massive-looking 2-10-4 Selkirk types at the White River Junction engine house.

GREEN MOUNTAIN FLYER...

With a history of almost continuous financial distress, Vermont's Rutland Railroad was an utterly charming, if obsolescent, carrier whose ways reflected unhurried rural steam railroading of the early 20th century through the early 1950's. Unsurpassed in picturesque appeal, but otherwise a poor third in the three-way competition with Central Vermont and Delaware & Hudson for the daytime passenger trade between Montreal and Boston-New York, was Rutland's *Green Mountain Flyer*. (Left) The weathered walls of Rutland's Bellows Falls, Vermont, roundhouse are reflected in the placid waters of the Connecticut River as the Boston-Montreal section of the *Flyer* gets underway on a magnificent October day in 1949. Hand-

somely groomed K-2 class Pacific No. 85 (Alco, 1929) had just emerged from heavy repairs in the company's Rutland backshop. (Above) Northbound on Boston & Maine rails from its New York Central connection at Troy, K-1 Pacific No. 82 speeds the *Flyer* through the junction of B&M's Troy and Mechanicsville lines at Johnsonville, New York, in the spring of 1950. (Below) 4-8-2 No. 92 delivers the southbound *Flyer* to its New York Central connection at Troy Union Station in May 1949. From 1929 until the first diesels arrived on the property in 1950, the only new Rutland locomotives were four of these L-1 Mountains delivered by Alco in 1946.

WHERE SUPER-POWER WAS BORN . . .

Treading Berkshire Hills grades laid down by pioneer railway builder George Washington Whistler more than a century before, Boston & Albany Berkshire No. 1420 bursts out of State Line Tunnel, just west of the New York-Massachusetts line, with eastbound tonnage for the New York Central's arm into New England. Modern steam power was born here in the Berkshires in 1925 when the Lima Locomotive Works sent its new experimental high-horsepower 2-8-4, the A-1, east for trials on B&A's rugged profile. So impressive were the results that by 1930 there were 55 near duplicates, named for the Berkshires they had conquered, on the B&A roster. For half a

century Pacifics in a variety of classes and sub-classes worked Boston & Albany passenger schedules. In the scene at top right, one of them emerges from State Line's 562-foot westbound bore with local train No. 2211 in the summer of 1948. Soon after the introduction of New York Central's celebrated 4-6-4 Hudson in 1927, subsidiary Boston & Albany got 20 of its own, distinguished by short tenders, smaller drivers, and oversized sand domes in deference to B&A's shorter line and decidedly non-water level profile. (Right) Class J-2b Hudson No. 608 approaches State Line with eastbound train No. 508.

14

ALCOS AND AN RDC . . .

New Haven was an early convert to main line dieselization, utilizing a fleet of 2,000 h.p. Alco road units as dual service power. A pre-war batch of 60 DL-109 units was augmented in 1948-49 with 27 of Alco's post-war PA-1 units. At the left, two of the flat-nosed PA-1's lead southbound train 29, the Boston - New York *Gilt Edge*, through Wickford, Rhode Island, in June of 1959. Beginning in 1952 New Haven acquired one of the largest fleets of Budd Rail Diesel Cars in North America. (Above) RDC No. 25 lays over at Woods Hole, Massachusetts, in 1959 after completing a run from Boston down the Old Colony Line to the Cape Cod port, where connections were made with steamships serving Martha's Vineyard and Nantucket Island.

ALLAGASH
AND THE GREAT BORE . . .

In 1934 and 1937 Boston & Maine took delivery of ten handsome P-4 class Pacifics from the Lima Locomotive Works. In a happy return to railroad custom of the 19th century, each was given a name of regional significance selected by New England school children. (Above) On a rainy afternoon in 1948 P-4-a Pacific 3711, *Allagash*, heads the Montreal-Boston section of the *Ambassador* at White River Junction, Vermont, where B&M assumed responsibility for the train from Central Vermont. Visible just beyond the locomotive is the Junction's archaic "highball" signal; in New England the old ways sometimes died hard. (Right) A westbound B&M freight for Mechanicville, New York, emerges from the 25,081-foot Hoosac Tunnel in 1949 behind a mix of F-3 and FT diesels. Some 22 years, 195 lives, $14 million, and endless controversy after its construction was first proposed, the Fitchburg Railroad's great bore was finally holed through the Hoosac Range of the Berkshire Hills in 1873. Now B&M's Fitchburg Division, the Hoosac Tunnel Route affords the Yankee carrier a crossing of the Berkshires fully 600 feet lower than that of the rival Boston & Albany.

2. LINES EAST

Traversing what represents both the industrial heartland and the most densely populated region of the North American continent, and touching the great seaports of the Atlantic seaboard, the railroads of the Eastern states transport a density of traffic that is unparalleled in American railroading. It should follow, then, as a matter of course, that in moving the East's intense volume of freight and passengers Eastern railroading should account for a goodly number of railroading superlatives.

The East's recently merged Penn Central represents the world's largest transportation company, and even before merger with the New York Central the Pennsylvania generated more ton-miles of freight transportation each year than any other railroad, moved more passengers over its multiple track New York-Washington corridor than any comparable stretch of rail on the continent, operated the greatest electrified system in North America, and, indeed, moved a greater traffic behind juice than all the others put together. Transporting a commuter traffic of near-subway density, the Long Island moves a greater passenger count than any other American railroad. Until the decline of the "great steel fleet" in recent years, nowhere in American railroading was there anything quite the equal of the parade of long distance passenger limiteds the New York Central sent storming up the east bank of the Hudson every afternoon for decades on end. The great Eastern systems operate a mileage of four-, five- and six-track main lines that is unequalled anywhere else on the continent. And only in isolated instances outside the East can be found conveyer belt tonnages of coal and ore comparable to those transported as a matter of routine by such Pittsburgh-centered industrial carriers as Pittsburgh & Lake Erie or Bessemer & Lake Erie.

The superlatives are virtually endless, but these few examples should suffice to make the point.

With their origins dating to the very beginning of steam railroading in North America, the Eastern lines have generally remained in the forefront of the industry's technological pioneers and innovaters. It is perhaps an appropriate measure of the stature of Eastern railroading to observe that only the Pennsylvania could have ever laid claim to so audacious a title as "the standard railroad of the world" and that only another line, the New York Central, could ever have seriously disputed it.

Frequently independent in the extreme, the Eastern lines introduced memorable variety into the railroad scene. Until the diesel brought enforced uniformity, individuality was nowhere more evident than in motive power. Big enough to go their own way, both the New York Central and the Pennsylvania pursued highly independent steam power design philosophies. The results, in the form of Paul Kiefer's splendid Hudsons, Mohawks, and Niagaras, or the Pennsy's ranks of Belpaire-boilered K-4's, and duplex-drive T-1's and Q-2's, were with us well into the 1950's. When Pennsy opted for main line electrification it characteristically developed a line of juice power that was totally unlike anyone elses. Even the smaller Baltimore & Ohio produced a few remarkable experiments in steam before becoming the first major eastern road to plunge wholeheartedly into dieselization. And surely no road of comparable size ever equalled Delaware & Hudson for the unorthodoxy and experimentation that characterized its steam power.

Slow to dieselize, slow to forsake a traditional preoccupation with passengers, and sometimes slow to embrace such technology as Centralized Traffic Control and electronic yards, the major Eastern systems went through some trying times during the post-war years, until the likes of Young, Perlman, Symes, and Saunders took hold. It is perhaps symbolic of the resurgence of Eastern railroading in the 1960's that in 1966 a New York Central jet-propelled rail car established a new American railroad speed record, and that the Penn Central was readying its New York-Washington line for America's first regular 160 mph passenger trains.

18

Under the leadership of Chief Engineer of Motive Power and Rolling Stock
Paul W. Kiefer, one of the leading architects of modern steam power, the
New York Central System developed a memorable line of high performance
steam power that began with the J-1 class Hudson of 1927 and culminated
with the S-1 class dual service 4-8-4 Niagara of 1945. Massive in appearance, impressive in performance, the 235-ton, 6,600 horsepower Niagara
was widely regarded as one of the finest examples of the 4-8-4 wheel arrangement ever built. S-1b Niagara No. 6006 was a powerful argument in
the affirmative on a September afternoon in 1949 as the big 4-8-4 scooped
up a tankful of water on the fly as she raced through the Tivoli track pans,
New York-bound down the east bank of the Hudson with train 90, the
Chicagoan.

LOREE'S LOCOMOTIVES . . .

During the brilliant 1907-38 presidency of Leonor F. Loree, Delaware & Hudson embarked upon a remarkable era of steam power innovation and development which helped gain the anthracite carrier a stature in the industry out of all proportion to its size. In both new power and older engines rebuilt in company shops, D&H experimented with exceptionally high boiler pressures, compounding, and a variety of mechanical improvements in a quest for improved steam power efficiency. If few roads shared D&H's continuing enthusiasm for such wheel arrangements as the Consolidation or the Pacific, which remained the principal D&H freight and passenger power until World War II, such Loree era mechanical advances as tender boosters, roller bearings on driving axles and side rod bearings, and welded boilers were widely adopted.

Pre-Loree D&H power is reflected by Ten-Wheeler No. 558, shown above crossing the Hudson on the Troy-Green Island bridge in September 1948 with a summer-season-only extra section of the *Laurentian*, operating from Grand Central Terminal to Lake George. At the top of the opposite page Loree Pacific No. 652 passes West Waterford, New York, in the spring of 1949 with Whitehall-Albany local No. 4. One of three Pacifics built during 1929-31 in D&H's own Colonie, New York, shops, No. 652 carried its auxiliaries suspended between the frame members and sported uncluttered Continental lines in deliberate imitation of British practice. (Right) Pacific No. 604, a pre-World War I engine, achieved similar styling in a Colonie rebuilding. The 4-6-2 headed the southbound Montreal-New York *Laurentian* at Green Island, New York.

20

CHALLENGERS IN THE MOHAWK VALLEY . . .

On the eve of the second World War, Delaware & Hudson began the acquisition of a fleet of modern high performance steam locomotives, which by 1945 had reached a total of 15 K class dual service 4-8-4 Northerns and 40 J class 4-6-6-4 Challengers. If the Loree era reliance on relatively small power was gone, the new super power continued an unmistakable D&H style that was characterized by capped stacks, recessed headlights, and exceptionally clean lines. Above and at the right, J-95 class Challengers No. 1517 and No. 1519 pound up the 13-mile, 0.88 percent ruling grade out of the Mohawk Valley at Schenectady, New York, with 123 cars of westbound Susquehanna Division freight in the spring of 1950.

OVERLEAF

A decided bump in the otherwise largely gradeless profile of the former New York Central's "Water Level Route" between New York and Chicago is presented to westbound traffic by West Albany (New York) hill, where the Central main line turns away from the Hudson River Valley to cut across to the Mohawk Valley at Schenectady. In steam days helpers were required to boost westbound traffic up West Albany's 1.63 percent ruling grade, but most diesel-hauled trains were able to make the hill unassisted. With a fresh snowfall cloaking the Hudson Valley hills, a pair of 2,000 h.p. Fairbanks-Morse units takes the 17-car westbound *Empire State Express* up the grade on February 26, 1950.

STEAM ON WEST ALBANY . . .

In May 1948, the Central's new EMD passenger units appeared only on the road's premier trains, and steam power still dominated the action on West Albany hill. (Above) One of Paul Kiefer's magnificent Niagaras, S-1b class No. 6002, storms through a sweeping reverse curve midway up the hill with the westbound *Mohawk.* On the opposite page a westbound local bites into the grade with a pre-World War I K-11 class Pacific on the point and a chunky U-2d class 0-8-0 helper shoving mightily from the rear. At the top of the grade the pusher will cut off on the fly.

MOHAWK WEST AND THE *LAURENTIAN* . . .

Ideally suited to the largely gradeless New York Central profile, the 4-8-2 Mohawk constituted the backbone of the Central's roster of heavy steam power from World War I until dieselization. Altogether, Central acquired 600 of the versatile Mohawks between 1916 and 1943. Although most were built strictly as freight power, some 75 Mohawks delivered in 1940 and 1943 were designed as 80 mph dual service locomotives, and turned in some notable performances at the head end of heavy passenger trains until the advent of the Niagaras and diesels. (Above) Mohawk No. 2993, an L-2d class delivered by Alco in 1930, accelerates 135 cars of westbound freight out of Selkirk Yard near Albany, New York, in 1950. (Left) Boston & Albany Mikado No. 1226 performs pusher duties for the same train. Probably no other locomotive in the era of modern steam power enjoyed as wide an acclaim as the Central's magnificent 4-6-4 Hudsons, of which 275 were built between 1927 and 1938. At the top of the opposite page J-Ie Hudson No. 5339 backs onto the southbound *Laurentian* at Troy Union Depot, where the Central took over the Montreal-New York train from Delaware & Hudson. (Right) J-3a Hudson No. 5427 handles the same train through the interlocking at Rensselaer, New York, where the Troy branch joined the Hudson Division main line.

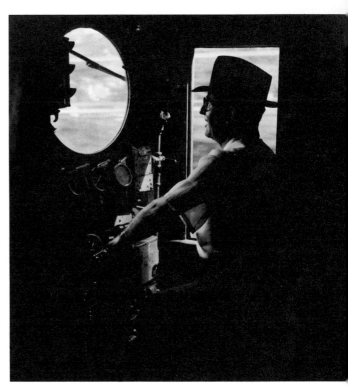

COMMUTER CARRIERS . . .

A characteristic shared by almost every major railroad serving the New York metropolitan area is an abundant, twice-daily traffic in commuters, moving to and from the market places of the city and the bedroom communities of the Connecticut, New York, and New Jersey suburbs. Two extremes in New York suburban traffic are depicted on this page. The principal New York commuter line, the Long Island Rail Road, hauls some 74 million passengers a year — one out of every four U.S. railroad commuters. The intense traffic typical of LIRR is represented by the photograph at the left above, taken from the rear car of an eastbound M.U. train on the six-track artery that connects New York's Penn Station with the Long Island's Jamaica hub. At the above right, a Long Island engineer operates a New York-Babylon M.U. train over the Montauk Branch. (Below) In a bucolic scene of rural New Jersey in 1950, Delaware, Lackawanna & Western 4-6-2 No. 1139 shows a clear exhaust as she heads local train 1120 through Andover on the Sussex Branch, enroute from Branchville to Hoboken, where passengers will board a Lackawanna ferry for Barclay Street in downtown New York. The N-5 class Pacific, one of four built by Schenectady in 1923, was equipped with the wide Wooten firebox that characterized the steam power of the eastern anthracite-burning roads.

PAOLI LOCAL . . .

For close to a century Philadelphians have regarded residence in the handsome suburban communities strung along some 20 miles of the Pennsylvania's main line west between Overbrook and Paoli as a prime cachet of social distinction. Ever since 1915, when the Pennsylvania electrified the line to Paoli with the 11,000 volt A.C. catenary that was to be a prototype for later electrification of the system's principal eastern lines, main line commuters have ridden to and from Philadelphia on the Pennsy's distinctive tuscan red, owl-faced multiple unit cars. Above, an M.U. local inbound from Paoli to Philadelphia's Suburban Station approaches the overcrossing of the Philadelphia Suburban Transportation Company's Norristown Division at Radnor in April of 1964.

READING'S COMMUTERS . . .

Sharing Philadelphia's extensive railroad-hauled commuter traffic with Penn Central is the venerable Reading Company, which has been transporting passengers between Philadelphia and its suburbs ever since the 1830's. Some 50,000 commuters a day ride the Reading, most of them aboard a fleet of over 150 multiple unit cars operating on a network of six electrified suburban lines radiating from Reading Terminal at 12th and Market Streets. (Above) A two-car train of 85 mph Budd Pioneer III M.U.'s accelerates out of De Kalb Street station in Norristown on a run from Philadelphia. The bridge overhead carries the Norristown Division of the Philadelphia Suburban Transporta-tion Company, which operates a rival electric service to Philadelphia via a connection with the Market Street elevated at Upper Darby. At the top of the opposite page, a single Budd car races northward from Philadelphia near Jenkintown on a mid-morning trip in 1964. (Right) Three types of Reading suburban equipment are displayed in a late evening lineup at Reading Terminal, Philadelphia. In the left background and at right are two of the steel and aluminum M.U. cars built by Bethlehem Shipbuilding in 1931-32 when Reading electrified its suburban lines. In between are a Budd RDC and one of the 1963-built Budd M.U.'s.

GG1 . . .

In 1928 the Pennsylvania Railroad announced the most ambitious main line electrification project in the history of North American railroading, and within the next decade 11,000 volt A.C. catenary had been activated over the New York-Washington and Philadelphia-Harrisburg main lines, as well as several other principal freight or suburban routes. Soon after the first section of the new electrification was opened in 1933, the Pennsylvania's motive power department set out to design a spectacular new electric locomotive of the 2-C+C-2 wheel arrangement for high speed passenger service. By early 1934 the prototype of the new GG1 class had been delivered for road tests, and so impressive were the results that over the next nine years Pennsy took delivery of another 138 similar units. Measuring 79 feet 6 inches between coupler faces, weighing over 230 tons, and capable of a maximum output of nearly 10,000 h.p., the magnificent 100 mph GG1's permitted a substantial acceleration of Pennsy passenger schedules and quickly captured the public fancy to a degree equalled by few other railroad locomotives. Here, GG1 No. 4877 lunges northward at Bowie, Maryland, in 1963 with a heavy Washington-New York express.

MAINLINER AT RADNOR . . .

One of the most enduring examples of the industrial designer's art must surely be Raymond Loewy's styling of Pennsy's GG1, which seems as fresh and modern in the 1960's as it did in the 1930's. One of the principal Loewy contributions to the GG1 design was the adoption of a smooth, arc welded carbody in place of the awkward-appearing riveted design of the prototype. Ever-youthful at the age of 24, GG1 No. 4890, one of 20 units delivered under a 1940 order, comes sweeping around a curve under the graceful catenary of the Pennsy's four-track Main Line at Radnor, Pennsylvania, in the spring of 1964, New York-bound with a heavy overnight express out of the West.

THE PIONEER B&O . . .

Not content with its distinction as America's oldest railroad, the Baltimore & Ohio has long maintained a position as one of the nation's most progressive systems. Thus, in the mid-1930's B&O, together with Santa Fe, pioneered the application of non-articulated diesel-electric power for road passenger service. B&O No. 50, an 1,800 h.p. box-cab locomotive built by Electro-Motive in 1935, was the first such unit placed in regular service. Two years later B&O took delivery of six streamlined, two-unit EMD EA's, which established the "bulldog" nose, twin engine, six-wheel-truck passenger unit format that was to dominate main line passenger dieselization in North America. (Right) One of the pioneer EA's, two-unit, 3,600 h.p. No. 54, accelerates the westbound *Capitol Limited* out of Baltimore's Camden Station in June 1948. (Above) Chicago's 1948 Railroad Fair offered such diverse modernity as a Central Niagara, C&O's touted coal-burning steam turbine, and GM's *Train of Tomorrow*, but the prettiest lady there, hands down, was B&O's 21-year-old P-7d President class Pacific No. 5304. The company's Mount Clare shops at Baltimore rebuilt and streamlined four of the Baldwin 4-6-2's for *Cincinnatian* service in 1946. By far the most numerous steam power wheel arrangement on B&O was the workhorse 2-8-2 Mikado. The most powerful of all B&O Mikes were the Q-4 class, built by Baldwin during 1921-23, which weighed over 163 tons and delivered a tractive effort of 63,200 pounds. At the right, Q-4 No. 4401 leaves a siding at Riverdale, Maryland, with a Potomac Yard-Baltimore freight after clearing an eastbound passenger train on a rainy day in 1946.

3. ATLANTIC SEABOAR

South of the Potomac, railroading along the Atlantic Seaboard is dominated by just three systems.

Operating largely along east-west axes, the two great Pocahontas coal haulers, Norfolk & Western and Chesapeake & Ohio, roll their massive tonnages of West Virginia soft coal down across Virginia to the Tidewater car dumps on Hampton Roads. For both, passengers are a negligible consideration, while general freight traffic is substantial, but in either case the preoccupation is with coal tonnage.

Paralleling the coast south from Richmond, where they connect with the Richmond, Fredericksburg & Potomac's bridge to the lines of the North, the magnificent dual raceways of the recently merged Atlantic Coast Line and the Seaboard Air Line railroads speed such urgent traffic as perishables from Southern farms and Florida groves to Northern markets, or the annual

hordes of Northern vacationers who flock to the Florida beaches by the streamliner-load.

A distinguishing feature shared in common by the two predecessor lines of the new Seaboard Coast Line has been this remarkably durable long-haul passenger trade between the cities of the East and Florida. Ever since the affluent of Boston, New York, and Philadelphia discovered the wintertime delights of the Florida beaches and watering places in the 1880's, the winter season passenger trade has loomed large in the fortunes of the two leading Atlantic Seaboard lines. Indeed, the premier Florida train, the winter-season-only *Florida Special,* has operated since 1888, a longevity that ranks it as one of the several oldest named limiteds still operating on the North American continent. Beginning in the late 1930's both Seaboard and Coast Line introduced diesel-electric power and

At the left above, purple-clad Coast Line diesels totaling 6,000 horsepower have just taken over the 20-car *East Coast Champion* from Richmond, Fredericksburg & Potomac at Richmond's Broad Street Station. (Above) Chesapeake & Ohio's 230-ton, all-roller-bearing 2-8-4 Kanawha No. 2756 typifies the modern steam power that characterized the Pocahontas roads until dieselization.

OUTH

streamlined rolling stock to the Florida trade, and commenced a general upgrading of track, roadbed, and signalling that transformed the once leisurely carriers into two of the major speed merchants of the postwar period. Lavishly supplied with service innovations and extras, vigorously promoted, and operated according to service standards of consistent excellence, the Florida trains of the now merged lines have remained relatively invulnerable to the decline that has affected much of the long haul passenger market in North America over the past two decades. Even today, Seaboard Coast Line schedules no fewer than four "Land Cruise" through streamliners daily between New York and Florida points during the winter season, not to mention a considerable number of lesser trains.

The excitement along the lines of the Atlantic Sea-

board South was by no means confined to 90 mph, stainless steel streamliners in the postwar era, for both Coast Line and Seaboard approached a highly competitive freight traffic situation with equal enterprise. Heavily dependent upon a traffic in such high-rated and urgent — and hence vulnerable to highway competition — commodities as Florida fruits and vegetables, both carriers applied prodigious quantities of diesel-electric horsepower to their crack merchandise, perishable, and piggyback schedules. By the beginning of the 1960's both roads had accelerated their freight schedules sufficiently to gain a position in the front rank of North American fast freight operators, and for several consecutive years during the early 1960's Seaboard Air Line managed to post the fastest freight timing on the entire continent.

ONE NIGHT AT FLORENCE . . .

A division point, junction of lines radiating in four directions, and the halfway point between New York and Miami — Florence, South Carolina, is the center of intense activity on the former ACL main line. Typical of the peak freight and passenger traffic that hits Florence in the hours after dark are these scenes of Coast Line activity one August night in 1957. (Above) Southbound No. 1, the *East Coast Champion*, was allowed just five minutes for a crew change and servicing of its three-unit diesel and 20 cars. (Above Right) Yard lights glinted from stainless steel car sides as 6,000 diesel horsepower accelerated No. 1 south over the Charleston District. (Below Left) Florence passengers boarded No. 2, the northbound *East Coast Champion*. RA Tower operator L. S. Guyton (Below) controlled traffic south and west from Florence. On the page opposite, six diesel units and 121 cars made up Richmond-Jacksonville time freight 109, ready to roll south from Florence yard.

41

41

HAVANA SPECIAL...

Operating on a more leisurely schedule than the streamliners, Coast Line trains 75 and 76, long known as the *Havana Special* but more recently identified on public timetables as the *Gulf Coast Special*, provided convenient daytime service to main line ACL points between Richmond and Jacksonville. (Above) The northbound *Havana Special* whips under a signal bridge approaching the Charleston, South Carolina, station stop in 1957. (Below Left) No. 75's lead diesel unit gets its face washed during a Florence (South Carolina) servicing stop. Engineer J. F. Brunson has a firm grip on his cigar (Below Right) as he wheels southbound train No. 75 at 90 mph.

SEABOARD LOCAL . . .

Before merger, and before ACL moved its headquarters to Jacksonville, Wilmington, North Carolina, was very much a Coast Line town. Rival Seabord Air Line got into Wilmington, too, via a branch line from Hamlet. At the right, the now-vanished daily Seaboard local from Charlotte, North Carolina, No. 14, has just arrived at the Wilmington station behind a GP-7 on an August afternoon in 1957. (Below) The same equipment returns to Charlotte in late afternoon as No. 13. The bascule bridge, shared with Coast Line, carried SAL over the Northeast Cape Fear River.

TORPEDO NOSED MOUNTAIN . . .

Among the very limited number of entirely successful attempts to streamline the steam locomotive must be included those of Norfolk & Western. Both the road's celebrated class J 4-8-4's of the early 1940's and a modernized series of U.S.R.A.-design class K-2 4-8-2's of post-World War I origin received similar treatment at the hands of N&W's Roanoke shopmen. Encased in a sleek torpedo-nosed shroud, and finished in a conservative glossy black with a single tuscan red stripe, the J's and K-2's conveyed an unforgettable image of power and speed. Above, Brooks-built (1919) K-2 Mountain No. 122 departs Richmond's Broad Street Station in 1957 with a *Pocahontas* connection that will operate to Petersburg via Atlantic Coast Line. In the background a three-unit ACL diesel is ready to depart with the southbound *Everglades.* The two views on the opposite page at right, taken at N&W's Norfolk Union Station shortly before its abandonment late in 1962 for more modest quarters adjacent to the road's freight yard across town, seem to typify the declining state of railroad passenger service in the 1960's. At the top of the page opposite, the next to last train to depart from Norfolk Union Station was the Geep-hauled Christmas Night 1962 version of trains 21-15, the combined *Cannon Ball* and *Cavalier* for New York City and Bluefield, West Virginia, respectively.

Unlike many regions of North America, where a few dominant features establish an essential character, railroading in the great Middle West defies summarization. If, for example, Eastern railroading is dominated by the multiple track and intense traffic of Penn Central, or the West by vast distances and hostile geography, the railroad scene of the Central States is characterized only by diversity.

Midwestern freight traffic is dominated by no single commodity, as is the Pocahontas region by soft coal, the Northwest by lumber, or the Canadian prairie by grain. Rather, the waybills of Midwestern freights are as diverse as American railroading itself: ore from the Mesabi, coal from Southern Illinois, grain from the Dakotas, meat from the packing houses of Omaha and Chicago, steel from the mills of Gary, automobiles from the factories of Detroit — the list is virtually endless.

In recent times Midwestern passenger traffic has generally reflected enterprise and innovation that have been unequalled by any save a handful of systems in the Far West and the Southeast. Birthplace of the streamliner, the Midwest adopted it more widely, and with greater enthusiasm, than any other region. Throughout three decades of streamliners the lines of the Central States have dominated Donald M. Steffee's celebrated annual tabulation of passenger train speed, and, with only few exceptions, a Midwestern line has posted the fastest North American timing every year since the mid-1930's.

Chicago, the hub of Midwestern railroading, is second only to New York City for commuter traffic volume. In the two postwar decades the Chicago based lines have approached the vexing problems of commuter service with a remarkable aggressiveness that has produced such innovations as gallery cars, push-pull trains, automated fare collection, and, most remarkable of all, black ink in the commuter books.

Nowhere was Midwestern diversity more apparent in the postwar decades than in the motive power departments of the region's carriers. Although the successful road diesel was born in the Midwest, and Midwestern roads were among the pioneers of road dieselization, steam power nonetheless lasted long in the Central States. Rosters of aging Moguls, Ten-Wheelers, Pacifics, and Mikes, well adapted to the modest requirements of the Midwest's bountiful mileage of branch lines and lightly-trafficked secondary routes, frequently lasted well into the 1950's. Modern steam power was no less evident. Super-power Mountains, Berkshires, and Hudsons were commonplace, but the high performance 4-8-4 was easily the favorite. Well-suited to Midwestern traffic demands, sizable fleets of Northerns were employed by almost every major road for both heavy passenger and fast freight work.

Articulateds were uncommon in the Midwestern states, yet paradoxically what was perhaps the most notable performance of steam power was that afforded by the massive 2-8-8-4 Yellowstones of Minnesota's Missabe Road, which continued to roll ore trains in excess of 18,000 tons down to the ore docks at Two Harbors and Duluth until the end of the 1950's. It was both one of the grandest shows in a century and a quarter of North American steam railroading and the last major operation of steam power on the continent.

As a small boy gazes in fascination, an Illinois Central Mikado departs Madison, Wisconsin, with the daily way freight round trip from Freeport, Illinois, in June 1953. No. 3969 was one of two rebuilt Vicksburg, Shreveport & Pacific 2-8-2's that regularly worked the Iowa Division's Madison branch until the arrival of Electro-Motive Geeps in the mid-1950's.

IOWA DIVISION STEAM . . .

Beginning in the late 1930's Illinois Central's Paducah (Kentucky) Shops carried out an extensive rebuilding program that provided the railroad with a roster of modern high performance steam power sufficient both to carry IC through the extraordinary traffic of World War II and to hold off dieselization for nearly a decade longer than on almost any other railroad. IC's most powerful steam locomotives were 20 Central type 2-10-2's of the 2800-2819 series, rebuilt at Paducah during the early 1940's from lighter 2-10-2's delivered by Lima shortly after World War I. Until diesels took over in 1955 the big 2-10-2's were assigned to Iowa Division tonnage. (Above) Central type No. 2804 accelerates eastbound freight past Rath Tower at Waterloo, Iowa, in August 1949. A "one-of-a-kind" Paducah rebuild was Mikado type No. 3962, shown at top right outbound from Madison, Wisconsin, with the Freeport (Illinois) way freight on a raw January day in 1949. The former Vicksburg, Shreveport & Pacific 2-8-2 shared Madison branch duties with the similar ex-VS&P Mike pictured on the preceeding page. At the right, an operator at Waterloo's West Tower hands up a Form 19 order to the crew of a 2-8-2 on a westbound way freight.

49

GREEN DIAMOND GEEPS . . .

Slow to dieselize its freight traffic, Illinois Central skipped
the cab unit phase of freight dieselization entirely. Instead,
IC began buying Electro-Motive's GP series hood units in
1950. By 1958 there were enough of them on the roster
to eliminate the last IC steam power. To many, the writer
included, the angular, utilitarian Geep of the pre-chopped
nose era represents an unsurpassed example of handsome
and functional industrial design. Surely none looked better
than the IC version. Devoid of either bright colors or
ornate paint schemes, IC Geeps were finished in a glossy
jet black, relieved by just the right amount of white strip-
ing, bold engine numbers on each side of the hood, and a
crisp green diamond herald on the cab sides. Above, a
pair of IC GP-9 units climb out of the Mississippi River
Valley at Dubuque, Iowa, with the solid reefer consist
of westbound dispatch freight 77. At left above, Mississippi
Division Traveling Engineer T. C. "Tip" Nelms wheels
the Geeps of New Orleans-Chicago freight NC-6 across
western Tennessee. At the left, the engineer of Council
Bluffs-Chicago CC-6 scoops up a Form 19 order from the
operator at Portage, Illinois, operating over joint trackage
shared by IC with Chicago Great Western and the Burlington. At the right, train CC-6 is ready to move out of
the Fort Dodge, Iowa, yard behind three GP-9's on an
autumn night in 1957.

IC SUBURBAN...

Second only to the Long Island Rail Road in U.S. commuter volume is the Illinois Central's electrified suburban operation at Chicago. Possessed of a superb physical plant, IC Suburban moves an annual traffic of more than 26 million commuters on a system of only 38 route miles. The principal IC Suburban route, which parallels IC's main line for some 29 miles from the Chicago Loop to suburban Richton, varies from six to two grade-separated tracks, all of them devoted exclusively to suburban traffic. Double-and single-track branches provide multiple unit service to South Chicago and Blue Island. At left, a southbound M.U. brakes to a halt beside the platforms at Roosevelt Road with Chicago's splendid Michigan Avenue skyline in the background. At the right, a Blue Island Local Express heads west on single track just after leaving the Suburban main line at 116th Street in Kensington.

CITY OF NEW ORLEANS AT KENSINGTON . . .

A superb example of the daytime coach streamliner — and one of America's fastest trains — ever since its inaugural run in April of 1947 has been Illinois Central's *City of New Orleans,* which daily runs off the 921 miles between Chicago and New Orleans on a breakfast-to-midnight schedule. Above, on a July morning in 1964 IC train 1, the southbound *City,* comes hurtling past the Suburban platforms at Kensington, powered by a trio of Electro-Motive E units led by E-8 No. 4031. Further south, on the 125 miles of the Champaign District between Champaign and Centralia, the orange and brown streamliner will hit a top speed of 100 mph over one of the fastest stretches of roadbed on the North American continent.

THE *LAKER* AT GRAND CENTRAL . . .

One of the best surviving examples of 19th century railroad terminal archi-
tecture in North America is Chicago's Grand Central Station, designed by
architect Spencer Solon Beman and erected in 1888-90. Above, under Beman's elegantly proportioned train-shed, a Pullman porter waits in the full
dignity of his calling to greet passengers aboard his car on the Soo Line's
Laker, soon to depart on its overnight run to Superior and Duluth. Until
it vanished from Soo timetables in January of 1965, the leisurely, congenial
Laker was a favorite with knowing travelers in the upper Midwest.

PACIFIC 2719 AT SUNSET . . .

One of the last outings for steam on the Soo Line Railroad was a splendid excursion of Twin Cities enthusiasts into rural Wisconsin in the autumn of 1958 behind the Soo's handsome H-23 class Pacific No. 2719, one of six engines built by Schenectady in 1923 that were both the Soo's heaviest and newest 4-6-2's. At left, backlighted by a late afternoon sun, extra No. 2719 rolls westward after rejoining the Minneapolis-Sault Sainte Marie main line from the Ridgeland Branch at Barron Junction, Wisconsin. Below, No. 2719's engineer, Norm Jacobson, studies a train order on the trip east from Minneapolis.

THE FRIENDLY SOO . . .

Soo, now freight-only, was never a major passenger carrier. Lacking routes of adequate passenger potential, Soo passed up the streamliner era; instead continued to operate rolling stock of pre-World War I origin on schedules to match. Even at that, Soo equipment was well maintained and comfortable, its dining service exemplary, and its employees displayed a folksy friendliness that was altogether genuine, and the railroad enjoyed a well earned esteem among its limited passenger clientele. Typical of Soo passenger trains — and the Soo countryside—is the view above of westbound Minneapolis-Enderlin (North Dakota) local No. 5, photographed near Loretto, Minnesota, on a frigid Thanksgiving Day in 1958. The Electro-Motive F-7 unit that powered the train was Soo's only concession to the technological advances of mid-century railroading. More typical of Soo passenger power was Pacific No. 2719, shown at left leading a 1958 excursion train over a timber trestle on the Ridgeland (Wisconsin) branch. On the opposite page the Pacific storms upgrade with the same 10-car special near Osceola, Wisconsin.

SOO FAST FREIGHT . . .

In the highly competitive transportation market of the upper Midwest the Soo Line has
carved out a place for itself by operating one of the better fast freight services in U.S.
railroading. In the photograph at the top of the opposite page a pair of GP-9 road
units accelerates across the Soo's Mississippi River bridge in 1958, outbound from
Minneapolis' Shoreham Yard with the 121 cars of the *Western Soo-per,* a hot shot fast
freight for Western Canada and North Pacific Coast points. Above, in the early morning hours of a June night in 1958 the F-7 road units of time freights 24 and 25, opposite
numbers in fast overnight service between Chicago and the Twin Cities, are serviced
at Stevens Point, Wisconsin. At the far left, the Soo's operator at Moose Lake, Minnesota, hoops up a 19 order to the conductor of a westbound freight extra. At left,
the crew of an ore extra, eastbound from the Cuyuna Range to Superior, Wisconsin,
doctors a hot box at McGregor, Minnesota.

AFTER DARK ON THE "LOUIE" . . .

One of the great railroad success stories of recent years was that of the Minneapolis & St. Louis Railway. Under the able management of receiver — later president — Lucian C. Sprague, the 1,600-mile M&StL was rebuilt from a decrepit streak of rust that emerged from a near record 20-year bankruptcy in 1943 as a first line contender for Midwestern freight traffic. In the scene above, two years before M&StL vanished as a corporate identity in a 1960 merger with Chicago & North Western, F-3 unit No. 400 leads a four-unit diesel about to depart from Minneapolis' Cedar Lake Yard with train No. 20, the road's crack overnight time freight over the 488-mile Minneapolis-Peoria main line. On the opposite page, gas-electric car GE-31 pauses at suburban St. Louis Park, just outside Minneapolis, enroute to Watertown, South Dakota, as train 13.

DAN PATCH LINE . . .

Minnesota's 61-mile Minneapolis, Northfield & Southern Railway is a descendent of a singular gas-electric short line that was named for the famous race horse and, in 1913, became America's first freight and passenger carrier operated exclusively with internal combustion motive power. In modern times MN&S has found prosperity as a bypass "bridge line" around the Twin Cities. In the view above a brawny MN&S center cab Baldwin transfer diesel thunders across the Minnesota River bridge with a southbound freight extra for the Chicago Great Western interchange at Randolph, Minnesota.

FORT FRANCES LOCAL . .

Canadian National Railways taps the Lake Superior "Twin Ports" of Duluth and Superior via a 172-mile subsidiary, Duluth, Winnipeg & Pacific. Until recent years a nightly DW&P local between Duluth and the CN main line at Fort Frances, Ontario, offered passenger connections to Canadian points. (Above) In 1956 the Fort Frances local still drew a heavyweight consist and steam in the person of CN Pacific No. 5133. (Right) By 1959 a single Rail Diesel Car had taken over the run. The Chicago & North Western diesel units at left headed a Chicago-bound overnight limited.

MINNESOTA SHORT LINE . . .

The Duluth & Northeastern Railroad is one of the few surviving remnants of a great turn-of-the-century logging railroad empire that blanketed much of the Northern Minnesota timberlands. Although D&NE trains once ran almost to the Canadian border over connecting logging lines, the railroad has been confined since 1941 to an 11-mile line whose principal traffic is pulpwood hauled from a Missabe Road connection at Saginaw to paper mills and other wood industries at Cloquet. The old ways died hard on D&NE, and such antiquities as arch bar trucks and hand-fired, Stephenson slide valve steam power survived into the 1960's. At the left above, D&NE No. 14, a handsome Consolidation outshopped by Baldwin in 1913, switches pulpwood cars at a Cloquet paper mill in 1958. At right above, the same locomotive takes water from an ice-festooned tank at D&NE's Cloquet enginehouse. (Left) An even older 2-8-0, No. 27, built by Pittsburgh in 1906 for the Duluth, Missabe & Northern Railway, steams across a country crossing in 1957 on the way into Saginaw from Cloquet. (Right) Journals are repacked on the arch bar truck of a D&NE flat car at Cloquet.

STEAM, STEEL AND MEN ON THE IRON RANGE . . .

Among the great steam locomotives of all time were the 18 Yellowstone type 2-8-8-4 articulateds that moved massive iron ore tonnages for the Duluth, Missabe & Iron Range Railway through the end of the 1950's. One of the half dozen most powerful steam locomotives ever built, a Missabe Yellowstone was a formidable machine that weighed in at 569 tons in working order, stretched fully 127 feet 8 inches between coupler faces, and developed a maximum tractive effort of 140,000 pounds. Working at full throttle a Yellowstone consumed some-

thing like 500 pounds of bituminous coal and evaporated a ton and a half of water every minute. The final ore season for Missabe steam power, and the last great steam operation in North America, came in 1959. (Above) M-4 class Yellowstone No. 228 is ready to roll 200 empty ore "jimmies" up to the Mesabi Range from the Proctor, Minnesota, yard on a May afternoon in 1959. In the views below are the men who ran her. At the left, engineer Ed App looks back for a highball. At the right, fireman John Shovein checks his fire through Butterfly fire doors.

THE CHALLENGER . . .

The locomotive that challenged big steam on the DM&IR was no ordinary diesel-electric. The Missabe found the brawn it needed for massive ore tonnages in Electro-Motive's 1,750 h.p., six-motor SD-9 model, and bought 74 of them between 1956 and 1959. Weighing over 190 tons and developing a maximum tractive effort of almost 97,000 pounds, the big maroon road switches were a worthy successor to the great Yellowstones. Here, a string of four SD-9 units totaling 7,000 h.p. heads a 170-car Two Harbors ore extra at Biwabik, Minnesota, on the Iron Range Division in 1958.

THE MISSABE AFTER DARK . . .

At the left, late on a May night in 1959 Yellowstone No. 228 waits to cross the scales at Proctor Yard with a just-arrived 190-car ore train grossing a phenomenal 17,468 tons. (Above) N class 2-8-2 No. 1303, a former Duluth & Iron Range locomotive built by Baldwin in 1913, is coaled at the Endion engine terminal in Duluth after completing yard switching duties. (Below) The Mikado is bedded down in the Endion engine house.

The Missabe Road's M-4 class 2-8-8-4 No. 228 has just backed onto 190 cars of iron ore from Minnesota's Mesabi Range at Fraser on the railroad's Missabe Division. Smokebox-mounted pumps exhaust furiously as the Yellowstone charges the train line. Soon Extra No. 228 South will be rolling toward Proctor Yard and the Duluth ore docks with a train grossing 17,468 tons and containing more than enough ore to fill a typical Great Lakes ore steamer.

73

Led by E-2 class Pacific No. 2911, one of 12 delivered by Schenectady in 1923, the North Western *Viking* rolls through the southern Wisconsin countryside near Waunakee in 1955. Rebuilt for 100 mph speeds, four of the E-2's powered the celebrated Twin Cities *400* from 1935 until dieselization in 1939.

In the several decades following the Civil War a powerful voice in the affairs of the agricultural Midwest was the farmers' organization known as the National Grange. A major objective of the "Granger" movement, as it became known, was to secure regulation of the railroads which provided the farmers' indispensable outlet to markets. To this day the agriculturally-oriented Midwestern roads which were principally affected by the Grange-backed regulatory legislation are referred to as the "granger lines."

Among the principal granger roads — railroad writer Frank H. Spearman called them "the big granger lines" — are the Chicago & North Western and the Milwaukee Road. The North Western was the first road out of Chicago — in 1848 — and the Milwaukee opened its first line but three years later. Between them the two lines played leading roles in building and developing the Great Midwest. Entwining northern Illinois, the entire states of Wisconsin, Iowa, and South Dakota, and southern Minnesota in a network of main lines and branches, the two Chicago-based roads dominate railroad transportation in much of the upper Midwest.

In recent years each of the two great Grangers has contributed much to the railroad scene. Together with the rival Burlington, the two lines were among the pioneers in launching the great passenger train revival of the 1930's, each in its own highly individual way. When Burlington ordered new diesel-powered *Zephyrs* for the hotly competitive Chicago-Twin Cities run, the Milwaukee responded with home-built *Hiawatha* streamliners, powered by a series of extraordinary 100 mph-plus Alco 4-4-2's. And North Western stole a march on both of them with the *400*, a fast-wheeling combination of souped-up E-2 Pacifics and refurbished "standard" equipment.

Before the two roads finally settled on diesel-electric power for their growing streamliner fleets, Midwestern travelers were treated to such steam power variety as elderly Pacifics and Ten-Wheelers, shrouded in streamlined hoods, and ultra-modern streamlined Hudsons on the head end of *Hiawatha* and *400* schedules. On the eve of *Hiawatha* dieselization Milwaukee's spectacular Hudson's were running the world's fastest-ever steam schedules, and Milwaukee steam power continued to operate mile-a-minute-or-better schedules through the end of the 1940's.

Before the bloom faded from the passenger market, Milwaukee went through three generations of West Milwaukee-built streamlined equipment, and pioneered the full-length dome, while North Western developed the "bi-level" streamliner. For its Chicago commuters North Western bought modern gallery cars, came up with the "push-pull" train, and showed how modern equipment and first-rate service could restore profits to suburban traffic.

5. THI

REAT GRANGER ROADS

THE NORTH WESTERN AT DEVIL'S LAKE . . .

Just south of Baraboo, Wisconsin, the Chicago & North Western's Madison Division enters the Wisconsin River valley through a spectacularly scenic glacial cleft in the Baraboo Hills at Devil's Lake. In the view above, E-2 class Pacific No. 2912 pounds through Devil's Lake State Park with the Chicago-Twin Cities *Viking* on an afternoon in the early spring of 1955. At the right, in a scene photographed from high on the lake's eastern escarpment, a single Electro-Motive E unit races past the lake with westbound train 519, the *Dakota 400*, in the fall of 1956. Installed in 1950 on the Chicago-Huron, South Dakota, run in a burst of postwar passenger enthusiasm, the *Dakota 400* lasted little more than a decade.

NORTH WESTERN PACIFICS . . .

In the twilight of North Western steam operation, well after such modern power as streamlined Hudsons and Class H 4-8-4's had been supplanted by diesels on main line passenger schedules, survivors of an abundant fleet of elderly C&NW Pacifics continued to head commuter and secondary passenger runs through the mid-1950's. On the page opposite, ES class 4-6-2 No. 660 roars through the Dane County countryside of southern Wisconsin on a September morning in 1955, shortly after leaving Madison with Chicago express No. 504. (Above) ES Pacific No. 617, one of two fitted with a green and yellow shroud in 1941 for *400* service, has drawn some appreciative on-lookers while waiting to depart from Madison's Blair Street Station with the same train. Until the end of steam operation, trains operating between Chicago and the Twin Cities via the secondary Madison line changed engines at Elroy, Wisconsin, a junction point between the North Western and its subsidiary Omaha Line. At left below, an Omaha engineer checks over heavy Pacific No. 504 at the Elroy roundhouse before forwarding the *Viking* on the last half of its Chicago-Twin Cities run. At right below, the *Viking's* conductor and the engine crew of E-2 Pacific No. 2905 chat during a leisurely halt at Madison in the spring of 1955.

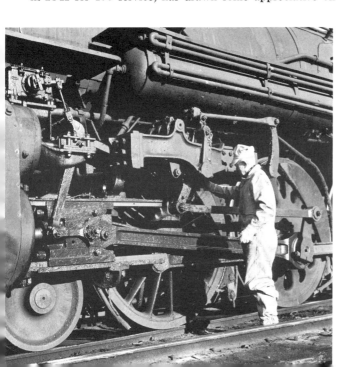

THE *400* AND THE BELOIT SWITCH RUN . . .

The North Western's eastbound *Twin Cities 400*, shown above, heads eastward out of Minneapolis for Chicago in 1959 over the Great Northern's splendid 2,100-foot stone arch bridge of 1883, whose 23 graceful masonry arches over the Mississippi River at the Falls of St. Anthony constitute one of the railroad wonders of the upper Middle West. At the right, local switching duties completed, an Alco road switcher accelerates southward out of Oregon, Wisconsin, in 1956, returning homeward with the Madison Division's "Beloit Switch Run," a daily way freight round trip operating between Beloit and Oregon via Footville.

THE TOWER IN THE LAKE . . .

Madison, Wisconsin, is a city virtually surrounded by lakes, with its downtown area located on a narrow isthmus between the two principal lakes of Mendota and Monona. The rival Chicago-Madison lines of both the Chicago & North Western and the Milwaukee Road reach the city from the south by means of embankments constructed across Lake Monona. Until it was replaced by a remote control installation in the mid-1950's, the mid-lake intersection of the two lines was guarded by the unique Monona Tower interlocking plant, whose facilities included a dock for the operator whose customary means of home-to-work transportation was a motorboat. At the left above, the *Capitol 400*, a Chicago-Milwaukee-Madison-Chicago schedule that vanished in 1950, accelerates past the tower in the fall of 1948, with the dome of the Wisconsin state capitol prominent on the Madison skyline. (Above) An L-2 class Baldwin Mikado heads past the tower coming out of the Milwaukee Road's West Washington Avenue yard in 1949 with a Chicago time freight whose early evening departure has been a diversion for Lake Monona front porch sitters for several decades. (Left) A North Western E-2 Pacific is wreathed in steam as it struggles out of town with Chicago express No. 504 on a ten below zero February morning in 1955.

MILWAUKEE PASSENGER POWER . . .

In 1934, when the Burlington announced an order for a pair of *Twin Zephyr* streamliners for a new daytime Chicago-Twin Cities service, the Milwaukee Road was quick to meet the challenge. While the Burlington's new trains would be diesel-powered, the Milwaukee elected to stay with steam. An important consideration in the Milwaukee's choice of steam for its new *Hiawatha* streamliners was the demonstrated performance characteristics of its only modern high performance steam power, a fleet of 20 big class F-6 Hudsons delivered by Baldwin in 1930-31. In a 1934 speed test one of the Baldwin 4-6-4's hauled a train at a top speed of 103 mph and averaged 92 mph for a distance of over 50 miles. Soon afterward the Milwaukee placed an order with Alco for the first two of four

magnificent class A streamlined Atlantics, whose 7 foot drivers could roll a train at 120 mph. By 1938 the *Hi's* popularity sent the Milwaukee back to Alco for six class F-7 Hudsons, a streamlined, high-drivered locomotive that could match the exhilarating performance of an A with a greatly expanded consist. In the photograph at top left, class A 4-4-2 No. 2, displaced from *Hiawatha* schedules by diesel power, brings the *On Wisconsin* into Madison, Wisconsin, from Milwaukee on a winter day in 1948. (Left) F-6 Hudson No. 136 storms out of Madison with the Chicago-bound *Sioux* on a bitter January morning in 1949. (Above) F-7 Hudson No. 101 rips through Columbus, Wisconsin, with the eastbound *Fast Mail* in the summer of 1949.

HIAWATHA REAR END STYLES . . .

Between 1935 and the late 1940's the Milwaukee Road went through three sets of *Hiawatha* rolling stock of advanced and highly individualistic design, virtually all of it constructed in the railroad's own West Milwaukee shops under the able direction of the Milwaukee's master car builder, K. F. Nystrom. The original 1935 *Hiawatha* was equipped with a tapered "beaver tail" rear end parlor car of altogether distinctive appearance. One is seen at top left on the opposite page, departing Milwaukee on a Madison train in March of 1948. A new set of *Hiawatha* equipment styled by Otto Kuhler and constructed in 1938 retained the distinctive beaver tail design for the rear end parlor car but afforded greatly improved rearward visibility. Fins above the windows provided a sun shade. The beaver tail parlor car *Miller* is seen at left on a

westbound *Hiawatha* at Milwaukee in 1948. Unsurpassed observation car visibility was provided by the Skytop Lounge cars styled by designer Brooks Stevens and constructed under the Milwaukee's postwar new equipment program. Four parlor Skytop Lounges were built for Twin Cities *Hiawatha* service in company shops, while six 8 double bedroom-lounge versions were constructed by Pullman-Standard for the new *Olympian Hiawatha*. One of the latter, *Marble Creek*, is shown above entering Minneapolis on the eastbound *Olympian Hi* in 1958. For a short period in 1947-48 while the Milwaukee was waiting delivery of the Skytop Lounges, the otherwise fully streamlined *Olympian Hiawathas* operated in the grand manner with standard open platform observation cars. One is shown at the top right on the opposite page.

Within little more than a decade of the opening of the Milwaukee's Pacific Extension to Puget Sound in 1909 the railroad completed one of the greatest electrification projects ever undertaken by a North American railroad. Made up of two independent sections through the Rockies and the Cascades, the project comprised a total of some 656 electrified route miles. Original Pacific Extension electric power was supplemented in 1950 with the purchase of 12- 5,530 h.p., 293-ton "Little Joe" locomotives originally built for the Soviet Union but never delivered. A common operating practice of recent years has found two of the big GE locomotives teamed in multiple unit with an Electro-Motive GP-9 diesel unit, a combination providing a total of some 12,500 h.p. and delivering a starting tractive effort of 250,000 pounds. On these pages such a combination is shown accelerating the 87 cars of westbound Chicago-Seattle time freight No. 263 out of Three Forks, Montana, in the summer of 1964.

GRANGER TONNAGE . . .

The biggest of the 50-odd 4-8-4 Northerns that represented the Milwaukee Road's only modern steam freight power were 40 S-2 class locomotives built by Baldwin between 1938 and 1940. Representing a combined engine and tender weight of better than 440 tons, and delivering a tractive force of almost 71,000 pounds, the S-2's had a big brawny appearance to match. In the photograph above, S-2 No. 208, one of 30 delivered in 1938, pounds through Columbus, Wisconsin, with main line tonnage late one summer afternoon in 1948. (Left) A pair of Alco road switchers is too long for its stall in the Madison, Wisconsin, roundhouse.

AFTER DARK AT PIG'S EYE . . .

Pig's Eye Yard, completed in the Mississippi River Valley just south of St. Paul, Minnesota, in 1956, is one of a series of modern automatic yards completed by the Milwaukee Road since the end of World War II. In the view above, tank cars roll down the Pig's Eye hump on a bitter cold February night in 1959. (Right) Diesel power waits for tonnage at the Pig's Eye engine terminal.

6. THE HILL LINES

One of the great railroad empires of all time was that assembled by James J. Hill, the one-eyed, Canadian-born tycoon who built the Northwest with rails of steel. The cornerstone of Jim Hill's empire was the decrepit St. Paul & Pacific Railroad, which Hill acquired with borrowed Canadian capital in 1873 and within two decades, as the Great Northern Railway, pushed all the way westward to Puget Sound — the first transcontinental to reach the Pacific without the aid of either federal cash or land grants. Within another decade Jim Hill had acquired control of the rival Northern Pacific and bought the Burlington, and soon afterward, through the jointly GN-NP-owned Spokane, Portland & Seattle, had tapped the once-exclusive Oregon preserves of the Harrimans' Southern Pacific. Of Jim Hill writer Frank Spearman said, "He is the last of our great railroad pioneers . . . There are no longer within our borders railroad wildernesses to be explored; of these Mr. Hill has thrown open the last."

Ultimately the Hill Lines empire comprised an aggregate network of some 27,000 miles in 19 states and two Canadian provinces, extending from Chicago to Denver and the Pacific Northwest, and from Canada south to St. Louis, Kansas City, and the Texas Gulf Coast. The waybills of Hill Lines freights reflected such diverse originating commodities as coal from the mines of southern Illinois, iron ore from the Minnesota ranges, the diverse agricultural products of the rich Red River Valley, grain from the Dakotas, Montana cattle, or timber from the forests of the Puget Sound country.

Although their merger ambitions of more than a half century have thus far been frustrated, but by no means abandoned, the Hill Lines have remained a closely allied group of dynamic, highly competitive railroads which have consistently maintained a position of leadership in railroad progress. In our time, for example, Burlington pioneered the diesel-electric streamliner with its *Zephyr* of 1934, built the first dome car in 1945, and showed the way to commuter profits in 1950 with the first modern gallery cars. GN, NP, and the "Q" were all among the major buyers of Electro-Motive's record-breaking FT freight diesel. And during the postwar era the Hill Lines, with such trains as the *California Zephyr*, the *Empire Builder*, and the *North Coast Limited*, developed the luxury, long distance "cruise train" concept to a level that has yet to be surpassed by any other railroad.

They called Jim Hill the "Empire Builder" and ever since 1929 the Great Northern's premier transcontinental has proudly carried the name. At the right, two Burlington E units lead Jim Hill's train across the Wisconsin River south of Prairie du Chien, Wisconsin, in 1957, eastbound to Chicago over the "Q's" magnificent speedway down the east bank of the Mississippi River.

HILL LINES' STEAM . . .

Although they were early converts to diesel-electric power, and indeed the Burlington pioneered its application to road service, steam lasted beyond the mid-1950's on all three of the big Hill roads. Show here is a sampling of the steam that lasted longest. (Above) One of the Burlington's great 0-5A class 4-8-4 Northerns — No. 5618 — races down the Mississippi River Valley near Newport, Minnesota, in the summer of 1958, Chicago-bound with a railway enthusiast special. At the right above, Great Northern switcher No. 843, a Baldwin 0-8-0 of 1918 origin, chuffs through the Superior, Wisconsin, yards a few days after Christmas of 1956 on the eve of total GN dieselization. (Right) The Northern Pacific's W-3 Mikado No. 1805 steams out of the Superior yard on New Years Day of 1957 with a Superior East End switch run from Duluth.

THE Q AND THE RIVER . . .

One of the most magnificent of American railroad journeys is that afforded by the Burlington's line between Chicago and the Twin Cities, which is at once a superbly engineered speedway and what is probably the most scenic rail route of the entire Midwest. For the better part of three decades Burlington trains operating over this route have posted North America's fastest point-to-point passenger schedules. From Savanna, Illinois, to the Twin Cities, a distance of almost 300 miles, the line follows the Missis-sippi River Valley, whose splendid scenery has been viewed from Burlington Vista-Domes for more than 20 years. At the left, westbound No. 21, the *Morning Zephyr*, swings past Lake Pepin in the Mississippi not far from Maiden Rock, Wisconsin, on an overcast June day in 1958. Two E units lead an eight-car consist that includes no less than five domes. (Above) Two of the Burlington's original FT road freight diesels of 1944 thunder across the Wisconsin River south of Prairie du Chien, Wisconsin.

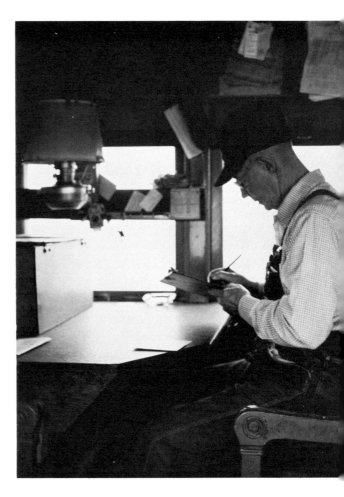

DOODLEBUG COUNTRY . . .

Before World War II the gas-electric motor car or the mixed train, providing a link with main line junctions or urban places, was an almost universal fixture of branch line railroading in rural America. While their like had largely vanished elsewhere, a considerable number of unhurried gas-electric "doodlebug" and mixed train schedules continued to ply the Northern Pacific's extensive North Dakota branch line network until the end of the 1950's. (Above) NP gas-electric car B-21, operating as Fargo-Streeter train No. 139 over the Fargo & Southwestern branch, has paused at the stucco station at Lisbon, the seat of Ransom County, on a spring day in 1959. (Top Left) Mail, express, and milk are loaded on and off the same train at Verona, North Dakota. At the right, milk waits for loading into the arch-windowed combine of Jamestown-Oakes mixed train No. 154 at La Moure, North Dakota. Up ahead freight is off-loaded from the train's l.c.l. "peddler" car. At the far left loaded cream cans are lifted into the combine's express compartment, and at the left the train's conductor does some paper work while the mixed makes its leisurely way from La Moure to Oakes.

THE *BADGER* AND THE GRAND FORKS LOCAL . . .

For many decades the favored mode of travel between the Twin Cities and the Twin Ports of Superior and Duluth has been aboard the Great Northern's *Badger* and *Gopher,* which operate morning and late afternoon round trips over the 160-mile route on brisk schedules. At the top of the opposite page, frost has coated the trees in white on a March morning in 1958 as the southbound *Badger* approaches the Nemadji River a few minutes out of Superior. At the left, the fireman on the same train leans out to snare a form 19 order at Central Avenue Tower in South Superior, Wisconsin, where the *Badger*

returns to GN rails after running over the Northern Pacific from Union Station in Superior. Of lesser import to Twin Ports travelers was the now-defunct Duluth-Grand Forks local, which is shown above wreathed in steam after arriving at Superior Union Station at dawn on a frigid November morning in 1957, eastbound from Grand Forks and Bemidji to Duluth. The train's locomotive — No. 181 — was one of a small GN fleet of pre-GP series road-switchers, built by Electro-Motive between 1939 and 1946, which were essentially elongated 1,000 h.p. yard switchers equipped with train heating boilers.

MAINSTREETER AND CONNECTION . . .

Backing up the crack *North Coast Limited*, Northern Pacific trains Nos. 1 and 2, the *Mainstreeter*, concentrate heavily on head end business and passenger service to NP's lesser intermediate points. At the right, freshly painted in NP's handsome Raymond Loewy-designed green and white colors, F unit 6507A leads No. 1 west across the Minnesota prairie from Minneapolis in 1959. Rail Diesel Car schedules between Duluth and Staples (Minnesota) provide Twin Ports travelers with convenient connections for both of NP's transcontinentals. (Below) RDC train No. 55 makes an early morning departure from Superior, Wisconsin, on its way west to a *Mainstreeter* connection at Staples. Budd car B-41 is crossing GN tracks at Central Avenue in South Superior. At the lower right, South Superior agent Dan McDonald takes a train order at NP's Central Avenue station.

NORTH COAST LIMITED . . .

Ever since its inaugural run on April 29, 1900, the Northern Pacific Railway's *North Coast Limited* has represented one of the great names of overland transportation in North America. During the past two decades Northern Pacific has lavished enough new equipment, imagination, and service innovations on the train to develop the Vista-Dome *North Coast Limited* of the 1960's into an unsurpassed example of the luxury "cruise ship" long distance passenger train. Handsomely decorated within and without, the *North Coast* consist affords a choice of accommodations from coach seats to all-room Pullmans, provides ample lounge and dome space, and offers both a buffet meal service and a full dining car service that ranks among the best in North America. At the right, the domes of an eastbound *North Coast* skirt the toe of a wooded bluff in Wisconsin's Wyalusing State Park on an early autumn morning in 1956 as the train races over the last lap into Chicago on the rails of the Burlington's great Mississippi River speedway. (Above) *North Coast* stewardess-nurse Marilyn Sanden chats with passengers in the train's imaginatively decorated *Travellers Rest* buffet-lounge while No. 25 bores westward through the Minnesota night toward Puget Sound.

104

7. LINES WEST

Representative of the rugged scenery of western railroading are the two views on these pages. (Above) The rocky walls of Colorado's Glenwood Canyon are glimpsed from a dome of the *California Zephyr*, westbound over the Denver & Rio Grande Western. (Above Right) Challenger No. 3975 shoves mightily to assist eastbound freight X-1439 up Wasatch Mountain grades on Union Pacific's main line through Weber Canyon east of Ogden, Utah, in February of 1951.

For more than a century the railroads of the West have waged eternal battle against a hostile environment that comprises great distances, formidable geography, and the most extreme of climactic conditions. Motive power has always played a preeminent role in this struggle against nature, and the big, brawny locomotives that have characterized western railroading have long represented one of its most captivating features.

In the era of modern steam power the West produced such unforgettable designs as the massive 10- and 12-coupled locomotives of the Union Pacific and Santa Fe that could match or better the performance of more than one modern articulated. The 4-8-4 Northern was born in the West and was found on every major western line. The West, too, brought the articulated locomotive to a peak of development with such designs as SP's unorthodox cab-forward 4-8-8-2; the

UP-originated 4-6-6-4 Challenger which, after its introduction in 1936, became the most popular of all modern articulated designs; or UP's great 4-8-8-4 Big Boy of 1941, regarded by many as the all-time high water mark of articulated locomotive design.

The western lines were in the forefront of the diesel-electric revolution as well. Union Pacific's *City of Salina* of 1934 was a *Zephyr* contemporary, the joint C&NW-UP-SP *Cities* streamliners of the 1930's were among the earliest long distance diesel streamliners, and Santa Fe was among the pioneers in the employment of both road passenger and freight diesel-electric units. In more recent years western experimentation with such motive power diversity as gas turbines, diesel-hydraulics, and massive diesel-electrics incorporating as much as 5,000 horsepower in a single unit has guaranteed that the western railroad scene will remain a fascinating one.

CHALLENGER COUNTRY . . .

No modern articulated locomotive enjoyed a greater success than that of the versatile 4-6-6-4 Challenger design originated by Union Pacific in 1936. Fast and powerful, the high performance Challengers proved an ideal locomotive for moving heavy tonnage over the West's long distances and rugged profiles, and not infrequently proved equally adept at keeping heavy passenger schedules to time. By 1944 there were well over 200 Challengers at work on half a dozen western lines — as well as several eastern seaboard roads. UP, with a total of 105, had the biggest 4-6-6-4 fleet of all. Anywhere west of Cheyenne on the UP trail was Challenger country. At the left, a Challenger moves a freight extra eastward across the vast and desolate landscape of southern Wyoming east of Green River in the summer of 1950. (Above) Challenger No. 3930, one of UP's last 20 4-6-6-4's delivered in 1944, fights a sharp grade near Rock River, Wyoming, with eastbound tonnage.

UNION PACIFIC BIG STEAM . . .

In order to contend with the varied operating conditions of a system of nearly 10,000 route miles extending from the Missouri River to the Pacific Coast, Union Pacific employed one of the most diverse rosters of steam power in North America. To forward Overland Route tonnages over the vast distances of the Nebraska prairie, the railroad developed its own 4-12-2 Union Pacific type, a three cylinder machine of awesome dimensions that could develop a tractive force only slightly less than that of one of the road's 4-6-6-4 Challengers. (Above) Union Pacific type No. 9500, one of 15 built in 1930 for the Oregon Short Line, moves westbound tonnage across Nebraska in 1951. A wheel arrangement that roamed the entire UP system was the 4-8-4 Northern. Between 1937 and 1944 UP bought 45 of them; the last 25 equipped with 80-inch drivers that permitted 100 mph speeds with a train of 16 standard Pullmans. At the left, Northern No. 819 heads the eastbound *San Francisco Overland* at Green River, Wyoming, in the summer of 1949. (Top Right) Challenger No. 3965 heads a 59-car westbound freight extra near Rock River, Wyoming, in 1950. (Right) Articulated No. 3566, an aging Alco 2-8-8-0 of post-World War I origin, joins forces with Challenger No. 3942 to move 101 cars of westbound freight through Borie, Wyoming, on the celebrated Sherman Hill west of Cheyenne.

REDWOOD CARRIER . . .

Extending some 40 miles through the California redwood country from Willits to Fort Bragg, on the Mendocino coast, the California Western Railroad is a logging and lumber line that has found unexpected popularity as a tourist carrier through the combination of its magnificent scenery and quaint "Skunk" rail cars. At the left, "Skunk" M-300, an American Car & Foundry internal combustion rail car of 1935 vintage that had seen previous service in North Carolina and Utah, arrives at Fort Bragg as westbound train No. 6 in July of 1964. (Above) The same car, shortly after entering California Western service in the summer of 1963, waits in the Northwestern Pacific station in Willits after arriving from Fort Bragg as train No. 3. The Southern Pacific Rail Diesel Car was scheduled to depart a few hours later for Eureka, operating as the NWP's tri-weekly *Redwood*, itself a scenic run of rare distinction. At the right, campers offload supplies from the baggage compartment of the M-300 at a forest stop between Willits and Fort Bragg.

SANTA FE IN CALIFORNIA . . .

There is a considerable body of opinion that regards Alco's postwar PA series passenger diesels as the handsomest ever built. Without question, the boxy-nosed PA's never looked better than they did in the striking red, yellow, and silver "warbonnet" colors of Santa Fe, which was the first to buy the design in 1946 and, with a total of 44 units, had the second largest PA fleet. At the right, a three-unit PA winds up for the dash across California's Mojave Desert from Mojave to Barstow with the eastbound San Francisco section of the *Grand Canyon* in 1950. Easily the most enduring of all streamliner color schemes, Santa Fe's "warbonnet" design has remained unchanged over the three decades since it was first applied in 1937 to Santa Fe's original streamlined Electro-Motive E1A units which, except for a dozen B&O units, were the first streamlined road units built in EMD's new La Grange plant. (Below) A pair of E1A's roll a Los Angeles-bound *San Diegan* streamliner along the Pacific beaches at Del Mar, California, in July 1950. Until dieselization, the most numerous type of Santa Fe passenger power was the 4-6-2 Pacific, of which several hundred were built between the turn of the century and the mid-1920's. The most powerful of all Santa Fe Pacifics were a group in the 3400 class built by Baldwin in 1919, represented below right by No. 3444, about to depart from San Diego with Los Angeles local train No. 75 in July of 1949.

MOUNTAINS AND CAB-FORWARDS . . .

Few railroads brought more individuality to the design of their steam motive power than Southern Pacific, and seldom were the results more photogenic. Two examples at the above left, Mountain No. 4317 and cab-forward 4-8-8-2 No. 4257, accelerate the 15 cars of the Portland-Los Angeles *West Coast* out of San Fernando on the last lap of its run via Sacramento and the San Joaquin Valley line in October of 1950. Another example of the 77 4-8-2 Mountains built for SP by Alco or the company's own Sacramento shops during the 1920's is shown at the left heading San Jose commuter local No. 124 out of San Francisco's 3rd and Townsend street station in 1951. (Above) Cab-forward 4-8-8-2 No. 4198, an AC-8 class built by Baldwin in 1939, heads out of siding with eastbound Coast Line freight No. 830 after being overtaken by the *Daylight* at Oxnard in 1953. At the right, operator Minnie Lee Beissel takes a form 19 order for westbound Coast Line freight 1st-No. 829 in the spring of 1954 in the same Chatsworth, California, depot where noted railroad fiction writer Harry Bedwell once held down a similar job.

THE *DAYLIGHT* . . .

One of the great trains of the streamliner era — and one of the most successful — was the Southern Pacific's *Coast Daylight*, operated over the 470-mile Coast Line between Los Angeles and San Francisco. For many, the handsome red and orange *Daylight* was, quite simply, "the most beautiful train in the world." From the time of their inauguration in March of 1937 until the mid-1950's the *Coast Daylight* streamliners were almost invariably powered by the Southern Pacific's Lima-built GS class 4-8-4's; themselves perhaps the most famous class of Northerns ever built. One of the most successful of all streamlined steam locomotive designs, the GS 4-8-4's, oddly enough, were hardly streamlined at all. Fronted by a splendid silvered smokebox and solid pilot, and equipped with the "skyline" casing applied to several SP locomotive designs, the GS Northerns required only a modest bit of metal skirting below the running boards and an imaginative red, orange, and black color scheme to evoke an image of speed and power far more effectively than almost any of the variety of far more extensively shrouded streamlined steam locomotives of other roads. (Above) A GS-4 4-8-4 lays a light plume of oil smoke across the citrus groves of Santa Susana as 20-car train No. 99, the San Francisco-bound *Coast Daylight*, gathers speed for the dash down the Simi Valley to Oxnard and the Pacific. At the right, No. 4458, one of two roller bearing-equipped Northerns built in 1942 as class GS-5, heads Los Angeles-bound *Daylight* No. 98 down the Rincon, just north of Ventura on the Pacific shore.

Midway between San Francisco and Los Angeles the *Coast Daylights* encounter a sampling of mountain railroading at Cuesta Pass, which provides the Coast Line a route across the Santa Lucia Mountains between the Salinas Valley and San Luis Obispo. Here, GS-4 Northern No. 4450 and 2-10-2 helper No. 3699 charge into the Cuesta Pass grade above Santa Margarita, southbound to Los Angeles with *Daylight* No. 98 in January 1951.

8. THE GREAT MOUNTAI

ASSES

Southern Pacific cab-forward No. 4149, a class AC-6 4-8-8-2 built by Baldwin in 1931, eases the loads of a Coast Line extra down the 1 percent grade of Santa Susana Pass on the way into Los Angeles' Taylor Yard in August of 1950.

For the main line railroads of the West there is no easy route into Southern California to tap the rich traffic of the greatest metropolitan area west of Chicago. No matter from what direction they approached, the railroad builders of the West had to find a way over or through the rugged mountains of the Coast Range before spiking down their rails to the Pacific shore at Los Angeles.

Traffic to and from the East over Southern Pacific's Sunset Route, for example, moves over the San Bernardino Mountains via San Gorgonio Pass, which confronts eastbound traffic with a 23-mile helper district and no less than a 49-mile grade for westbound tonnage. The two rival transcontinentals, Union Pacific and Santa Fe, come over the mountains from the Mojave Desert via Santa Fe's Cajon Pass line, one of the most photographed stretches of railroad in North America. Between San Bernardino and Summit eastbound traffic through Cajon climbs almost 2,800 feet in 25 miles of 2.2 percent grade, while westbound traffic climbs some 19 miles of 1.5 percent between Victorville and Summit and then drops down into the Los Angeles basin on descending grades as steep as 3 percent. SP added a new dimension to the Cajon scene in July 1967 when traffic between the San Joaquin and Sunset routes began moving through the Pass on the new, 78-mile Palmdale Cutoff, built to bypass Los Angeles congestion.

Southern Pacific traffic moving over the Coast Line between San Francisco and Los Angeles gets its severest test on the 2.2 percent grades of Cuesta Pass, over 225 miles north of Los Angeles, but Santa Susana Pass, separating the Simi and San Fernando valleys astride the Los Angeles city limits, offers a 1 percent grade, a tunnel over a mile in length, and some of the West's most photogenic mountain scenery.

The most severe operating conditions of all, however, are encountered by SP's San Joaquin Valley line in Tehachapi Pass, which affords a route over the Tehachapi Mountains between the Valley and the Mojave Desert for SP and Santa Fe (which has traffic rights) tonnage moving between Northern California and Southern California or the East. South of Bakersfield the rails through the Pass climb 3,610 feet in the 50 miles to Summit and comprise grades as steep as 2.5 percent, no less than 14 tunnels, and the celebrated Tehachapi Loop.

On these and the following pages is presented a photographic sampling from three of the great mountain passes of Southern California — Cajon, Tehachapi, and Santa Susana — in the postwar years.

SANTA FE IN CAJON . . .

One of the pioneers in main line dieselization, Santa Fe was both the first to order Electro-Motive's revolutionary FT freight diesel and — with 320 units — the owner of the largest FT fleet, and Cajon Pass has echoed to the chant of V-16 diesels and the whine of dynamic brakes (an innovation suggested by Santa Fe) ever since 1941. In the scene above, 6,000 h.p. worth of F-7 units, aided by two FT helpers at the rear, emerge from the 379-foot Tunnel No. 1 with the 70 cars of eastbound extra No. 206 approaching Summit on 2.2 percent grade in the fall of 1950. At the left, a newer generation of Santa Fe freight diesels is represented by a mix of EMD, Alco, and GE low-nose hood units, leaning hard on the dynamic brakes as they descend the 3 percent grade from Summit with westbound freight in 1966. At the top right, three of the passenger-geared F-7's that Santa Fe has long favored for first class schedules swing around the curve into Summit in 1950 with the 14 cars of 1st-No. 24, the eastbound *Grand Canyon*. Close behind (right) No. 3735, an elderly Mountain of Baldwin '23 origin, storms up the west slope into Summit with the second of three sections of the same train.

UNION PACIFIC IN CAJON . . .

For several generations of train watchers the sharp curve just west of Summit in Cajon Pass has been a favored location. At the left, three 2,000 h.p. Fairbanks-Morse passenger units and 4-10-2 helper No. 5092, one of 10 Southern Pacific types delivered by Alco in 1925-26, bring Union Pacific's eastbound No. 2, the *Los Angeles Limited*, around the curve into Summit in September of 1950. In the two photographs above the 87 cars of UP's Extra No. 1629 East are hoisted up the 2.2 percent west slope of Cajon at Alray on a hazy fall day in 1950 by the combined efforts of 6,000 h.p. worth of Alco freight units on the point and 4-10-2 and 2-10-2 helpers at the rear.

SECOND 806 ON TEHACHAPI . . .

Regardless of motive power, one of the great shows of western railroading has always been the north slope of Tehachapi Pass, where prodigious combinations of locomotive horsepower thunder up out of the San Joaquin Valley with an almost ceaseless parade of Southern Pacific and Santa Fe freight tonnage. The long climb to Summit begins only a few miles beyond the Bakersfield yard limits, but the action begins in earnest at Caliente; in just 28 miles from Caliente to Summit the rails climb over half a mile. In the photograph at the left, SP cab-forward 4-8-8-2 No. 4255, the last of four locomotives in the 58-car second section of eastbound freight 806, bites into the 2.2 percent grade on the upper end of the big horseshoe curve at Caliente on October 14, 1950. (Above) Four Electro-Motive F-7 units, aided by a pair of Alco road switchers cut in behind the caboose, grind up the hill above Caliente not quite four years later with another second section of the same train.

FROM THE LOOP TO MOJAVE . . .

The most notable single feature of Southern Pacific's magnificently engineered Tehachapi Pass line is the celebrated Loop at Walong, where the line's builders tunneled through a narrow ridge, looped the track around a hill, and crossed back over the tunnel, gaining 77 feet of elevation in the long climb to Summit in slightly over half a mile of 2.5 percent grade. In the photograph at the left, the dynamic brakes of four Electro-Motive F-7 units ease the tonnage of westbound SP freight No. 801 around the Loop on the way down into the San Joaquin Valley in 1950. At the top left, on trackage above the Loop near Tehachapi, three Alco PA passenger units race toward Summit with Santa Fe's eastbound No. 60, the San Fran-

cisco section of the *Grand Canyon.* In the siding, Southern Pacific's eastbound freight 2nd-806 waits to follow with an AC-12 class cab-forward 4-8-8-2 on the head end. Tehachapi's arid southern slope, rising from the Mojave Desert, lacks the spectacular scenery of the north slope, but affords operating conditions that are by no means insignificant; between Mojave and Summit the rails climb almost 1,300 feet in a distance of just 17 miles. In the scene above, photographed just above Mojave in October 1950, Mountain No. 4321 and GS-3 Northern No. 4419 storm up the grade with the 15 orange and red cars of the combined *San Joaquin* and *Sacramento Daylights.*

SP STEAM IN SANTA SUSANA . . .

At the west end of the San Fernando Valley Southern Pacific's Coast Line encounters an abrupt obstacle at Santa Susana Pass, where the rails tunnel and snake their way across a cleft between the Santa Susana Mountains and the Simi Hills. While its grades are neither as long nor as severe as those in such locations as Cajon and Tehachapi, Santa Susana is possessed of a unique and rugged scenery that has long made it a favorite locale for railroad photographers. In the view at the left, de-streamlined GS-4 Northern No. 4437 has just emerged from Santa Susana's 925-foot Tunnel No. 27, on its way down into the San Fernando Valley with Los Angeles-bound No. 72, the *Coast Mail*, in September 1953. The summit of the grade over Santa Susana is reached within the 7,367-foot Simi Tunnel No. 26. In the scene above, AC-10 cab-forward No. 4225 has just emerged from the east portal, with the tonnage of eastbound 2nd-No. 834 still stretched over the crest of the pass in the tunnel behind her.

SP IN CAJON . . .

Surging upgrade through the San Gabriel Range over Southern Pacific's superbly engineered Palmdale Cutoff, a mix of four Electro-Motive units heads a westbound freight for the San Joaquin Valley Route near Summit in Cajon Pass in late 1967.

9. LINES NORTH

Although overshadowed in such traditional measures of railroad bigness as gross revenues, revenue ton-miles, or passenger-miles by such giants of U. S. railroading as the Penn Central, Southern Pacific, Union Pacific, or Santa Fe, the two great Canadian transcontinentals exceed any other systems on the continent in the sheer breadth and diversity of their operations.

In terms of total miles of line operated both Canadian National and Canadian Pacific far exceed the largest U. S. systems. CN, the larger of the two Canadian systems, operates nearly 25,000 miles of line — almost 6,000 more than Penn Central, the longest U. S. system. Extending from the Maritime provinces on the Atlantic to the Pacific Coast in British Columbia, both Canadian systems embrace a geographic scope unparalleled in the U. S., and represent the only true transcontinentals on the North American continent north of Mexico. The 2,900-mile runs of such transcontinental passenger trains as CN's *Super Continental* and CP's *Canadian*, and even longer freight train schedules, far exceed anything comparable in U. S. railroading. Highly diversified, each of the Canadian transcon-

In a scene typifying the vast distances of Canada's prairie provinces, three Canadian National Geeps grind eastward out of Winnipeg's Transcona Yard in August of 1959 with grain for the Lakehead ports of Fort William and Port Arthur.

tinentals operates such varied transportation and communication enterprises as steamship lines, airlines, truck lines, express services, telegraph systems, and hotels.

Although CN experimented with internal combustion power as early as 1928, steam power remained in substantial numbers on both Canadian transcontinentals until the end of the 1950's. For as long as steam lasted such Canadian preferences as Elsco feedwater heaters, enclosed vestibule cabs, the semi-streamlined contours of newer CP power, or the commonplace application of such wheel arrangements as the 4-6-2 to dual service roles, brought a distinctive charatcer to railroading north of the U. S. border.

If Canadian individuality was diminished by dieseli-

zation, it has by no means vanished. Even though Canadian diesel rosters represent almost exclusively the products of the principal U. S. builders or their Canadian subsidiaries, peculiarly Canadian conditions have produced a goodly number of units that have no counterpart on U. S. lines. Lending a new vitality to the Canadian scene during the 1960's was a new enthusiasm for passengers on the part of the government transcontinental — CN — that produced such diverse attractions as Reading's *Crusader* and Milwaukee Road full-length domes and Skytop Lounges refurbished for Canadian National name train service, ultra-fast *Rapidos* on the Toronto-Montreal and Montreal-Quebec runs, and highspeed gas turbines for the Toronto-Montreal run.

CANADIAN NATIONAL STEAM . . .

Two extremes in CN steam power are represented by the photographs on the opposite page. At the top left, Ten-Wheeler No. 1406, built before World War I for predecessor Canadian Northern, smokes up backyard clotheslines at Ste. Anne de Beaupre, Quebec, as it hurries up the west bank of the St. Lawrence with La Malbaie-Quebec train No. 175 in 1958. At the left, U-1-f class Mountain No. 6065, built by Montreal in 1944 as one of the last CN steam locomotives, steams away from a station stop at Merriton, Ontario, with Toronto-Buffalo train No. 102 in 1950. A cone-shaped nose, flanged stack, and skirted running boards gave the 20 U-1-f's a clean-lined appearance that set them apart from the utilitarian design characteristic of most other CN steam power. (Above) A steam plume stands out against an early morning sky as the safety valve pops on a Mikado waiting with a work extra at St. James Junction west of Winnipeg, Manitoba.

DIESELS IN THE WEST . . .

Although slow to begin dieselization, the two Canadian transcontinentals, once committed to internal combustion units, carried out a motive power transformation of their vast systems in barely a decade. Save for switchers and a handful of road units, CN remained all-steam until the early 1950's. Yet by the end of the decade steam had virtually vanished from the system's more than 24,000 miles. Typical of the diesels

that vanquished steam on CN were Electro-Motive F-7 units such as those shown at left, which headed a westbound freight extra out of Rainy River, Ontario, through the CP crossing at St. Boniface in Winnipeg, Manitoba, in August of 1959. (Above) A variety of CN diesel units is shown under overhaul in the system's Transcona Shops at Winnipeg, maintenance center throughout CN's vast Western Region.

CANADA AFTER DARK . . .

At the top left on the opposite page, CN's U-1-e class Mountain No. 6050 is shown just before a late evening departure from Winnipeg Union Station in the summer of 1959 with westbound train No. 9 for Saskatoon (Saskatchewan) and Calgary (Alberta). Only a few months later dieselization of CN's entire Western Region was complete. At the top right, Winnipeg servicing crews clean cab windows on the lead unit of westbound No. 1, CN's *Super Continental*, midway on its 2,916-mile transcontinental journey. (Left) Canadian Pacific's Winnipeg station is a flurry of activity late on a rainy summer evening in 1959. At the far left, westbound train No. 1, the stream-lined Canadian, is about to depart on the last half of its trans-Canadian journey. In the foreground, G3h class Pacific No. 2433 waits to follow the *Canadian* west with overnight train No. 43 for Moose Jaw, Saskatchewan. (Above) Montmorency Falls, Quebec, agent Charles Auguste Hardy hoops up a form 19 order to the engineer of CN Pacific No. 5061, inbound to Quebec from La Malbaie in July 1958 with Sunday-only train No. 173, jammed with weekenders homeward-bound from Murray Bay resorts.

WINTER IN ONTARIO . . .

Steam power still dominated Canadian Pacific's Ontario main lines and branches alike when these photographs were taken on a leaden March day in 1956. In the photograph on the opposite page, Pacific No. 2209 and Mikado No. 5171, both of pre-World War I origin, head out across the Grand River bridge at Galt with a westbound freight extra for Windsor. (Above) Ten-Wheeler No. 888, a 35-year-old D10g class built in CP's own shops, heads a branch line freight between Woodstock and Ingersoll. (Below) P2d class Mikado No. 5356 steams across a rural crossing between London and Thamesford with eastbound main line freight.

With a venerable (Pittsburgh, 1906) Consolidation in charge, a Duluth & Northeastern Railroad freight struggled up the 1.5 percent grade out of Cloquet, Minnesota, to the Missabe Road interchange at Saginaw on a sparkling November morning in 1957.